The Mary Poems

From Death to Burial

January 14 to August 8, 2015

R. David Drucker

The Mary Poems: from Death to Burial, January 14 – August 8, 2015

ISBN: 978-1-937721-31-2
Library of Congress Control Number: 2016940673

Published by:
Peter E. Randall Publisher
Portsmouth, NH 03801
www.perpublisher.com

Book Design: Grace Peirce

Back cover photo: Alan Ammann

The text of this book is set in Adobe Garamond Pro

Dedication

This slim volume was occasioned by the sudden death of my wife and
constant companion
Mary Jane Carter Drucker
Whose confirmation name was Veronica
On January 14, 2015 at 12:54PM,
Immediately following a heart stent procedure at
Wentworth Douglas Hospital, Dover, New Hampshire.

This work is dedicated to Mary in the hope that
Those who knew and loved her as well as
The wider general public may know her more fully.

R. David Drucker
Dover, NH

Contents

Marriage Vows

Exchanged 30 July 1983 at the
Northshore Unitarian Universalist Church
Danvers, MA

BECAUSE we love, respect, and cherish each other and have proved ourselves to one another in adversity as well as happiness, we have asked you to witness our pledge of mutual support and continued trust for the years of our lives remaining to us.

WE joyfully pledge to continue to give support and comfort to each other when it is hard as well as when it is easy, to prosper in each other's growth, to ease pain, and to refrain from causing any, to listen with our hearts' desires, and to follow with open eyes the path our love requires.

R. David Drucker   Mary J. Drucker
30 July 1983

WE BEAR WITNESS TO THIS PLEDGE OF MARRIAGE:
[signed by 39 witnesses]

To Mary, My Dearest Mary

From your Dave

Read at Mary's Memorial Service at South Church Portsmouth, N. H.,14/II/2015,
Valentine's Day.

"I love you, my baby, I would say
night after night, day after day.
"I know you do, but I don't know why,"
daily would be your reply.
Night after night, day after day
for more than thirty years we'd try
this delicate dance, our delicious bedtime ballet.
A touch to your nose, a tug at your ear
was not, you made it clear, your cup of tea . . .
but you let me do it to dispel my daily fear
that any day you might disappear.
"Can you roll over? Can you warm my feet?
Can you hold me tight and hear our hearts beat?"
          you always used to say.
You always used to say
you had many fish to fry, many tunes to play.
You knew for love to be, there must be heart,
compassion.

          And your heart is true, sincere—
          that's why I love you, loveable you!

Your stubborn, frightened heart never ceased to fight
for countless people longing to be free of fear
they caused themselves . . . mere fear.
They love you, too—that's why they are here today with you.

Night after night, day after day
"no pain, no gain" was such a heartless joke—
your genetic hand never failed to bite you—

"Jinx, we owe ourselves a coke!"
What's left, my love? Something to explain
why I can't complain. Ah. You, gentle soul,
still charm me in your garden of love and delight.

Snow Song

For Mary

To music by Duy Bui

Some soliloquy of snow
summons me homeward.

Some small, gossipy snippet
of incessant meaning pursues my passage.

Wistful traces of my past
sustain a whisper in the wind
of quiet desperation.

                    A disembodied
"oo oo oo eee" screamed by some
snowy owl from his distant tree
completes this snow-swept scene.

Yes, I'll miss the hiss of outdoor snow
when I've passed safely home,
but I lust to savor the insulating warmth
of your first, welcoming kiss!

[22/IV/2015, Earth Day]

Nostalgia?

Sometimes a wisp of curly hair
or the sight of a nearby stair
is all I need—yes, you were here.

But, when it came to hair, you didn't care
to have me touch it lovingly . . . not fair!

I know when you put one foot on the stair
to climb leg over leg, but didn't dare.

So what's the upshot here? You now can not
         care I want to share
these thoughts with you . . . you can no longer care
when I oversentimentalize the
         life we used to share
together.
               Most of all, you cannot stare
me down if I begin to drown
in senseless seas of tears, or clown
incessantly if you seem down.
How I wish you could still be here to chide
misreading you—too late for that, my dear.

[19-20/V/2015 revised 9/VIII/2015]

Walking Our Favorite Sandy Shore Without You

A Sea Song For My Absent Mary

I need your loving arms to enfold me.

I search for you along this sandy shore
      we shared so many near-forgotten years ago.
The rhythm of the restless wind,
      the waves' bright hiss, gently tousles me.
Terns do not spurn me, sandpipers inquire wordlessly,
      gulls screech reluctant greetings . . . you ignore
my soundless cry. Swift-breaking waves sigh
      their soul-less burbling on the waiting shore.
I hear a dozen greedy gulls implore
      "feed me, feed me, I want more," but you ignore
      my hungry cry: "don't die, don't die".
Stay here by me, share this sandy shore
      one more time with me. Let's explore
      this windswept wilderness once more. Let's restore
      just one more fleeting touch, once more share our secret store,
      our upwelling thirst for one another.
                        This shore,
      so heartless, raw without you, cannot pour
      out sweet longings you always poured out to me.
This fickle wind only whispers out of habit, no more
      the breath of love we breathed together—we were as one
      those many years ago. We soothed our jangled fears as one.

It's clear this lonely sea and unforgiving sky
      can no longer satisfy. My eager heart
      longs only for you, my love, my Queen
      of the Sea, now unable to parse for me
      the fearful mystery of life without you.

I know why you do not answer me—
   I could not save you, my love,
     and now I'm lost—
     left to toss and break upon the shore—
     nothing left of us but memories
of loving this sanctuary, this mystery,
       this wild, untamed, unforgiving sea.

The air we breathed together,
   the secret sequestration of our hearts shared
     in loving wonder,

      is no longer strengthened by this wild,
unforgiving shore.
     [19/V/2015]

Wahsakayu:te<u>se</u>'—The Thunderers—April

A poem to Masie Shenandoah, Wolf Clan Mother of the Oneida Indian Nation

Beloved by Mary as a fellow champion of justice
July 12, 1932—December 2, 2009
In honor of her passing and in memory of her strength

MAY HER STRUGGLE TO BUILD THE ONEIDA NATION NEVER BE FORGOTTEN

Through west-facing windows in my log wall
I look out to you spring, summer, and fall.
For many years I've gathered strength as bouts
of lightening flicker on your corn-crowned ridge
backed first by thunder, then by rain.

                                        Can sprouts
like me find strength now that you're not about?
Your restless spirit stirs as Spring returns
wordless among the endless rows of new
maidens flaunting their fresh-faced regalia.

New this year, you, age-old hill, are sporting
a now silent body who does not rise
to greet the new-day dew
nor deign to spread her greening skirt to wave
greetings to the kindly faced Thunderers.

Though every other new-grown maiden gave
Thanksgiving for the ancient ones who save
them from a thirsting worse than death, they crave
to raise themselves to brand-new heights of growth—
you cannot. Holding to your hidden lair . . .
For you—no growth, regalia to amaze
the wandering Thunderers as they gaze
upon ranks of thirst-crazed maidens.

                                        A day's
sudden rapid changing of moistures stays
the need to seek a deeper, hidden source
of sustenance.

                    The rapt Thunderers graze
your life-affirming presence with a force
so gentle . . . yet it cannot stay your rage
to re-proclaim a more-cathected age,
reviving a once-lost will to engage
our Nation, to re-awaken . . . a rage
to live again in peace, justice and strength
until we once again attain One Mind.

May this crop last seven generations
to heal our broken Oneida Nation

                    [27/V/2015 revised 9/VIII/2015]

I, Bumblebee

I think that I will never see
a bumblebee quite as busy as me,
a creature ceaselessly ready to be
swept up by the latest mystery—
aware at any time I'm free
to stop this frantic, busy pace, free
to contemplate the mystery of you,
of me, of us, our mindful common destiny
that now is still.

                             The daily race
is always to the swift . . . I don't now care.
. . . We can no longer race together.
I race alone but never lose my tether
to you, still grip hard no matter the fetter
of busyness raging in me.

                         No matter my inner weather,
it's me, the busiest bumblebee,
buzzing, flowerless, my love, for you

                    [7/VI/2015]

Missing You One Rainy Night

To Mary

When I think of all the hours I couldn't sleep
counting persistent troubles instead of sheep
until I felt weary . . . it's not too great a leap
from there to dreaming dreary thoughts seeping
past mental screens I thought would keep
compartmented without a mumbling peep
forever, the rest of my life.

                                       How can I keep
from wringing every single tear I weep
on my sodden crying towel contained,
isolated, unconnected, constrained?

Always-existing never-ending source
of all my pent-up grief, no one can force
a cure for this encroaching theme but me.

If only I'd defy my destiny,
heartlessly release my heart, not weep,
but steel my heart . . . make it struggle free
from the heartless tyranny of being me.

I cannot will my path to change without you –
our less-straight path commands my loyalty.

Without you I will never be the me
you wished with all your heart would set you free.

[14-18/VI/2015]

The Double Rainbow

A Memory of You at Dallas
To Diana

When at last we met at that rain-pelted door,
we hardly knew the life we'd share.

                                        Before

the timid thunder's unsurprising roar,
there had been lightening and other signs that more
was waiting in the wings to gently shore
up the pallid signs of fraughtful weather.

This shimmering beauty boldly built a tether
twinning us together in our grief.
We both remembered you at once, together
shared a spark of instant longing . . . whether
for you or for us . . . and sealed it with a kiss.

Then a double rainbow blessed us paramours;
its twice-blushed hues inspired all our love.

By sharing only you we found our double bliss.

[15-18/VI/2015]

To Mary, As You Watch Over Me At Night

January to August 2015

My true love views me from a sky-blue box
nightly, clicking soundless beads of onyx,
counting her mindless rosary.

                              Flocks
of sleepless sheep slouch slowly towards the Styx,
immune to memory's comforts, heirs to shocks
of sudden panic—their silent bleat restricts
her attempt to shout my name, blocks
my fierce desire to hear her voice, and picks
the damnedest times to ignore me, locks
in lonely sand a once-full life, sticks
to a story of devastation that knocks
the stuffing from our cherished love.

                              Critics
will call this "overblown hyperbolics" . . .
"Grave where is thy strength, Death thy sting?"
these mindless, optimistic singers sing.

"Take heart, it's just the force of dialectics . . .
once you held her, now you don't . . . arthritics
have a funny way of living—switches
of mood aren't that uncommon—itches
don't always lead to scratches—patches
for pain and suffering often do the trick!"

It was not her back had the glitches
that tore my true love from me, but her heart
that wouldn't start . . . not orthopedics,
hot patches, not tender loving tricks
could start again her hopelessly tattered heart,
could resist Death's tireless, heartless tricks.

My Veronica, yours no longer to suffer fools gladly
                    who tried to cure you badly.

Neither now no longer can you cure me.
Sadly, I still love you, dearest, madly.

[29/VI/2015]

Still Addicted After All These Years

To Mary

I'd walk a mile for one of your mild smiles!
If only this camel weren't so dry-mouthed,
so parched from lack of drinking at the well
of your still-remembered eyes still casting spells
only in my longing heart.

                              Yes, wiles,
amazingly enough, are still your stock in trade–
and me, that one in a million, still your lover,
still retaining that need to keep you wild.

Inside my throat, that weary, certain catch
betrays everything I want—why can't you live
as long as I have breath to draw you in?
Why can't I savor all the luscious flavor
of your death-defying kisses?

                              Files
from those too-sophisticated actuaries
prove it should be me, not you, succumbs
to an addictive need to have you here.
Despite my plea for just one final puff,
there is no live-sustaining breath from you.

[2/VII/2015]

Four and Twenty Sorrows

Sing a song of loneliness—

    optimists needn't apply,

        only those who shake their fists

            defiantly to the sky.

Only those whose questionings

    are given no reply

        are the folks I'm singing to

            unless, of course, they die.

[9/VII/2015]

ON ENTERING TRINITY CHURCH, YORK HARBOR, MAINE, FOR A JAZZ CHOIR CONCERT

For Mary

Briefly heeded, a hint of incense freed
a need to plant an establishmentarian seed
in my scheming brain to ease the pain
that limns my inmost thoughts since losing you.

All of a once an inner choir intoned
an hundred nameless, soaring High Church hymns.
Once voiced, their scores informed mine inner eye,
sang themselves in mine innermost ear,
pleased my new, immutable, quavering,
inmost thoughts, on pitch, unwavering.

I loved those inner, non-visible signs
of an outward and spiritual grace,
a quickened slowing of my frantic pace,
my inmost chatter concerning the Devine,
which otherwise would ceaselessly incline
to replicate, increasingly, my whine.

But wait! This choir's music will be jazz!
Although the remnant incense flows, there's no
restless, unredemptive doubt to grow
metastasized deep in the heart of me.

In plainest words—there'll be no litany
remind me of my maladaptive show
of certain knowledge gained so long ago –
pain fades with every happy, soulful tune
that seems so right, though all the words be wrong.

Not High Church hymns, but you, becomes my song!

[26/VI/2015—17/VII/2015]

On Visiting Pine Hill Cemetery, Dover, NH

Seeing Our Joint Headstone in Place 9-11/VII/2015

I visited our last forever home
today, my love. It seemed inconsequential,
tiny. But, oh, how expressively vast
the vista from our minute yard! A burst
of frolicking foliage will whisper
sweet nothings in our non-existent ears.
This rustling cornucopia of cool
will constantly refresh our memory-parched
bodies, shield us from the incessant sun
that beats the life from those less fortunate,
those whose forever homes forever bake
in shadeless regions of our neighborhood.
How fortunate are we to share our fate
together—almost greedy in our shady
final resting ground.

Our spirits will calm
themselves continuously in this space –
our forever home we'll share together.
Forever blessed, we'll share this common place
eternally entwined, amazed by grace.

My Mary's Memory Palace

Mary's memory palace is a home
of many treasured attitudes whose rooms,
here on the deck, I can re-imagine—
make images of—what's on the walls?
No fancy, filigreed framing, nothing
gaudy, just basic necessary stuff
to live a life in . . . maybe a bit rough . . .
no crenelated peaks of gingerbread
for roof combs—just a special space where love
can invent a way to grow a slow-paced,
warm, unsophisticated, heart-felt grace –
more than enough to ease the daily blow
of all the outer world's uncaring show.

Where is that world of half-remembered dreams
filling my over-active brain with schemes
of layout, color, use? I never seem
to remember because, thinking of you,
all thoughts of logic, order, neatly spaced
infinities of possibilities,
lacking your inimitable presence,
become unthinkable.

                    Without your face
here before me . . . I cannot think, can't plan,
can't give this haunted memory house some order.
I can't think straight enough to straighten out
what is where, what is good and true, what is right
for site remembering . . . I see your hair,
your eyes, your gestures, and know these, not rooms,
are what I have to work with. You're not here
to guide me through your mansion, only tears
of sadness smooth my way from room to room
to final tomb. It's hard feeling my way
along the gloomy corridors of love
remembered, them dismembered.

                              Now, I'm lost,
become chartless, face-blind . . . as once you were.

No need for memory mansions now, my love.
With just our legacy of longing left,
we need no schemes for homes, however deft.

               [7-15/VII/2015 revised 10/VIII/2015]

On Driving Past WDH

The Uppermost Right-hand-most Window of the Central Avenue New Wing's Façade

I just passed by the window where you stayed
not so long ago against your will.

Many were the days we stayed together there
joking, reading, no matter what the weather
outside that giant window. We played together –
Sudoku, Jumble, endless rounds of Tetrus -
whiled away the hours.

      I left you only once
or twice, but hurried back to rub your feet
or hands or limbs to warm them up—still
they often chilled again, as tethered
to your monitoring equipment,
you could not leave your room . . . but your bed . . .
a different matter. I could lead you on,
watch, even stay with you until the dawn
crept coyly through the windowpane again.
Another night successfully endured!
Then . . . operation's done, your life's assured!

Tonight, driving past your former window,
I remember another time and place,
another smaller, less hotel-like space –
your face, limned with weary lines from worry,
telegraphing your gnawing, growing fear:
"Will I recover?" "Will I get out of here?"

You waited, bright in the glare of the sun,
to be wheeled off the floor, assigned a date
with destiny you never would have kept
had you known the truth.

                                    Surely, you'd have wept
as I do now full half a year away,
reliving, as do I, the mystery
of why I said, "Break an artery"
rather than, "Take good care, my love, don't cry . . .
I'll see you soon again, my love, goodbye."
You'd see I really thought that you and I
would meet again to laugh and cry together
when you awoke and cast away all worry –
healthier, if not wealthier nor wise.

Instead they made me see that you are dead
upon the bed we shared for just one night –
unsatisfied, devoid of all delight,
we had no time to share.

                              It's not right
that I'm still here and see you. The sparkling light
through the window recalls that other night
when hope was bright and future plans were quite
a possibility, and hope of flight
from pain accomplished—not this hopeless sight.

                    [10-11/VII/2015]

Completing a Half-Year Hitch of Death at Sea

To Diana

What can be done with you and what with me
on this sad, sixth month anniversary
we share together?

                    Of course, we are free
to cast emotion off. Our Odyssey
could overcome our anchored destiny,
could carry us from this deep mystery
of chaos, weakened strength. Our pent-up grief
could save us from foundering on a reef
of remembered regrets. We remember,
so such a voyage is improbable –
and, really, not even worth the trouble
to plot a course for such a fantasy.

Time and tide don't wait for any woman.
One hundred eighty-one days are now gone
since our beloved sailor lost her song
forever in the howling of a gale
riven by tone-deaf ocean birds who rail
at crass intrusions.

               One by one they hail
each other when they see a distant sail –
ours will not soon be on their horizon . . .
but hers . . . what every raptor relies on –
low resistance, lack of guile, weakened heart.
Those cagy birds pounced quickly without fuss
and snuffed our gallant sailor's life dead out.
No more was heard from her, no sound let out,
no longed-for song, not even a brief shout
from her, but they and we let out a shout
of pain heard 'round the world.

               The word is out . . .
no more can we share her life together,
we can only share our memories of her,
our love confined to cherished memories . . . her.

        [14-15/VII/2015 revised 10/VIII/2015]

32

To Mary

I've got a little secret I will share
with you now . . . it's our anniversary,
Mary, and I don't know what I will wear,
where I will go, or how I'll know enough to care
enough for two.

                              I'm just a bit wary
of sharing this. Yes, many truly care—
I see it in their eyes, catch it in their voice,
feel it in the tender touch their fingers
brush against my palm once they've squeezed mine

                              Choice
no longer comes easy to me. Singers
sing, preachers preach, teachers teach, joy lingers
in the messages these bards of hope voice
full-throated, earnestly . . . is it my choice
yet, or ever? I cannot say. My voice
is cracked, my throat parched. Am I a singer
still—extending joy to the afflicted,
comfort to the uncomfortable?

                              Dare
I find joy in weaving musical spells
to charm the darkest depressions others
feel—and cure my heart without you by my
side? Dare I write a Northern Harmony
to reconcile the savage dissonance
deep within my grieving heart?

How to start?

Light the candle once again. Read our vow
of forever love . . . you're still here somehow.

[26/VII/2015]

To Those Times That We Can't Get Back: We Meet

With apologies to Mary Goldthwaite-Gagne and Artstream

Now is one of those times, July twenty-ninth,
one day to go before I can't get back
our years that were, our life that was . . . our life.

Was it the lilt in your voice or the choice
of words you carefully crafted so strife,
the ever-present, betrayed not a word
when you understood I was not ready
to answer you in measured tones, in steady
rhythms—quantifiable emotion . . .
No, I wasn't ready nor were you. Talk
was far beyond our capability.
Gestures covered inscrutability.
We stood long and long, mutability
was our watchword. Silent, raw emotion
flashed between us, spawned a full-blown ocean
surge, rocking us to our very cores. Lone
pangs of longing, incapability,
wordless silence grew our unacquaintance
into sudden, brilliant, flowing love.

We felt, all of a once, a love above
all understanding—oceanic
love, trust, compassion, then sudden panic.

Our mutual wordless admiration
burst into our endless ocean song that never
more ceased to flow no matter how clever
our punster selves cast verbosity
on our deeper wordless need to be
free to swim the depths of our unbounded
love—free to scheme our dream, unfounded
in reason, all day long . . . 'til, astounded,

30

we talked away the night fully grounded
in who we were and what we did believe.

Now, on thirty-two eve, I talk the talk
we used to talk together, but can I
walk the walk we shared together? Not I.

Though hardly up to walking, still you walked
as I, now hardly up to talking, talked
away the night 'til now. The gigantic
void your disappearance, your non-appearance,
has opened in my heart has not been filled.

                                                  I cannot say I'm thrilled

to never see you face to face. I walked
so many crooked miles, so long ago
it only seems like yesterday, to know
the pain you knew can never be let go
as long as I remember who you are . . .
helps me keep compassion for us.

                                                  The scar

of losing you is nothing I'll forgo
until I join you soon, Mary, to go
on one great oceanic swim again.
                           [29/VII/2015]

Lighting One Final Candle Together

On Our 32nd Anniversary

Geraniums . . . roses . . . hydrangea starts
to flower for us, cure our aching hearts,
however temporarily. We greet
our love in all its glory and its need.

From your onyx box you watch the flame, hear
the vows we wrote each other to outfox
ourselves, keeping our hearts aware of blocks
to the happiness we'd share free of shocks
we'd later share . . . like this . . . our silent day.

You cannot read with me . . . you cannot stay
attached, engaged, all set to play tonight
from now to break of day.

                              A silence locks
your non-existent lips. This silence rips
my grieving soul . . . an empty feeling grips
my all-too-conscious heart. You will not start
to drift towards sleep nor take your future part
in everything we'd share, my dearest heart.

[30-31/VII/2015]

Veronica's Heart Breaks

What a poor thing my life is without you,
my sweet, unhearing, but not uncaring,
soul.

    Now, where can you be, my golden girl,
my brave, no-nonsense warrior woman,
my darling Veronica?

        Still saving
me unbidden.

        At last I know you're freed
of the savage scourge of never-stayed pain,
incurable autoimmune syndromes –
some with well-known names and many nameless –
the constant war your fiercely battle-scarred
body endured your whole life is over.

Why you, my brave, destiny-cheated love?
Why can't it be me who always suffered?
I'd rather you than me lived free of pain.

It's such a grave injustice that I lived
day after healthy day and you could not.
Why must you have died with a legacy,
a litany, of wrongly working parts.
They never worked, not once, as they should have.
Final irony—a non-working heart –
you of all people, whose heart worked always,
faithfully, forever, worked for all
the many forced to face their fate, fickle
in their loyalty, yet served by your
welcoming arms and ever-cheerful heart.

What's left, my love? Something to explain
why I can't complain.

                              Yes. You, gentle soul,
still charm me in your garden of love and delight.

[3/VIII/2015]

Our Last Night Together

You in our pretty sky-blue onyx box and me, just behavin', savin' my
love for whom my heart defends and loves, for you

Last night it was John Stewart, gone after
sixteen years . . . and now you, love, tomorrow—
despite my sea of tears, despite laughter
only half-remembered—no more to know
the nearness of whatever you've become—
no more comforted by your still closeness
watching over me night after night, free
to say nothing yet still be near for me,
allow me to be the me you wanted
me to be, to always sing, undaunted,
melodies we cherished . . . our memories
sacred to us—our vaunted histories
shared through decades. These are not mysteries
but mysterious . . . constant presences
in our lives . . . better, worse, richer, poorer—
our basic parameters of being—
are thicker than water or family,
truer than a hitman's fatal bullet
no sooner in the chamber than fired.

But, frankly, without the physical you
we cannot build anything really new.
I do know I cannot give life to you
nor you to me.

                The end of conscious life
means endless playing, no more pain, no strife,
but also means you cannot be my wife—
gone's lovely you, who always is my life.

[7/VIII/2015]

Burial—August 8, 2015

Twixt Hiroshima and Nagasaki
tricks of perception fool and trouble me.
I think I see devastated city
landscapes beckon me—bleak scenes, un-pretty,
stretch limitless to a gray horizon.
Twisted, ash-filled buildings . . . once-loved houses . . .
lie lifeless, once-loved havens from the storm
of life's unexpected situations,
accommodating daily all routine,
suddenly interrupted forever
those unanticipated August days
not so long ago. . . a world turned fiercely
still, deadly still. No mindful breath was drawn
among the slowly dying sufferers
still living those decaying hours, still filled
with senseless, relentless, post-atomic
suffering. Yes, no redeeming meaning
illuminated that awful, blinding
flash that lasted just a fright-filled, heat-seared
moment forever fixed in countless brains.

Now here I stand. A hundred flowers bloom
final flashes of hope in endless love.
Our devastated band of shell-shocked, mute
survivors find their voice to praise your love
of us. We dead awaken once again,
though you, my love, remain in endless sleep.

[9/VIII/2015]

Map of Pine Hill Cemetery

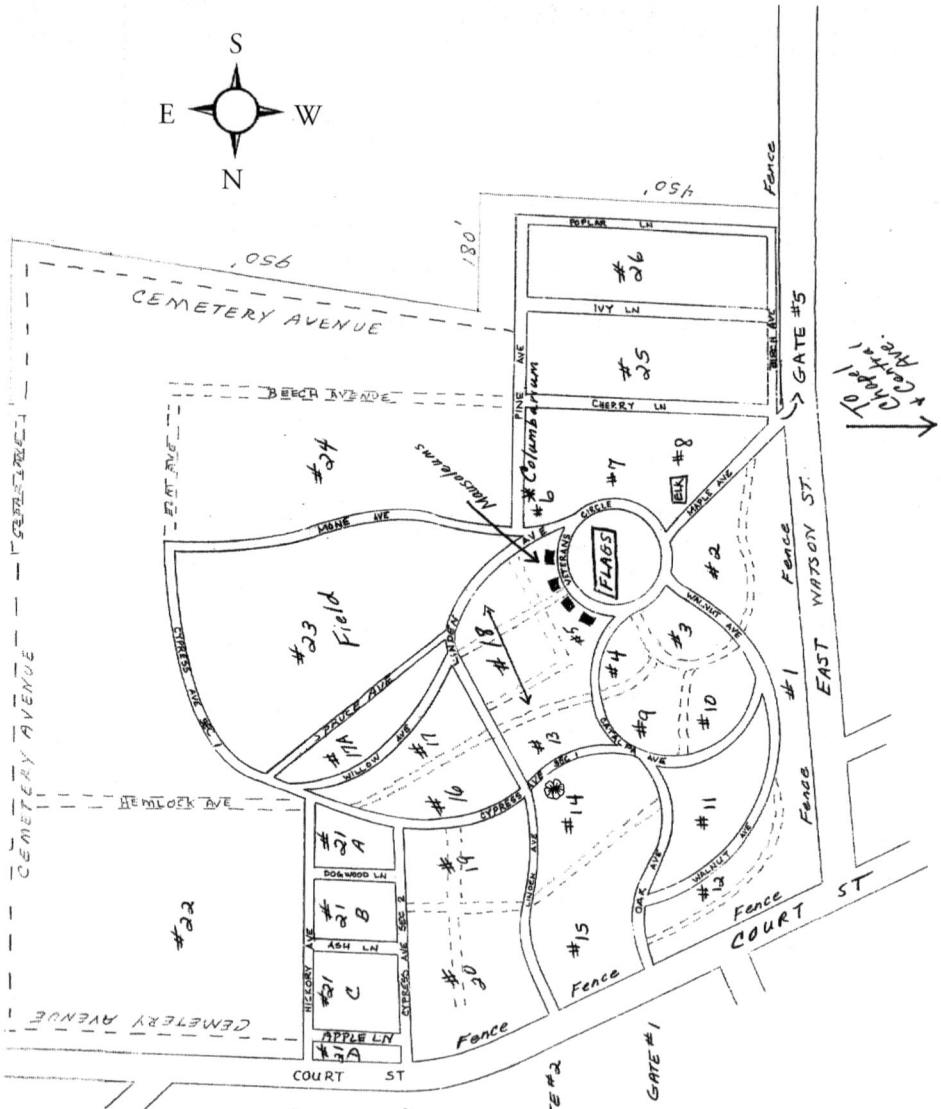

Pine Hill Cemetery Groups
✿ Group 14
Lot 17
Avenue Cypress
Graves 4, 5, 10, 11

Photo Gallery

Mary takes on the world - eyes wide open

Mary and Dave - New beginnings

Mary and Dave - Still lovebirds after all those years

Diana's wedding - Mary gives her baby away

Mary with Christopher - Diana's second child

Mary and Dave with Rachel - Diana's first child